Affirmations

for

Queens

Praise for

Affirmations for Queens
Tamara Skyhawk

"A wonderful new narrative to replace that internal negative self-talk. Tamara's affirmations are my new daily cheerleader… wonderfully positive, and compassionate words that align my Self with my life goals; easily, and effortlessly." – *Edna Pereira, MACP, Registered Psychotherapist, About Mind Mental Health Clinic*

"The antidote to a world that often tries to squash you down… quirky, fun, endearing and uplifting – just the pick me up you need!" – *Dr. Katarina Bulat, B.Sc., D.C*

"This book is like having your BFF, life and career coaches by your side all the time." – *Kathy Gorman, Sr. Marketing Consultant*

"Tamara keeps it REAL… pumping up the ups… supporting you through the downs… all while acknowledging the common humanity of being a QUEEN!"
– *Sharlene Louden, Care Owner, R.Kin*

Affirmations
for
Queens

99 Pep Talks for Self-Confidence,
Magnificence and Phenomenal Gloriosity

Tamara Skyhawk

*For all the PHENOMENAL Queens I've had the incredible privilege of being inspired and supported by – Edna, Kathy, Kat, the Kates, Liz, Shar, Jennie, Peggy, Jolene, Jane, Lisette, Sheila, Shira, Sol, Sam, Carla, Mom, Melissa, Mary, Natalie, Nuku, Jonathan, Rebecca, Shelley, Stacey, Jacqueline, Ros, Rae, Rose, Ashlee, Christine, Eliza, Xanthe, Natalia, Lisa, The Lynns, Kristina, Ashley, Erin, The Amandas, Carolyn, Donna, Kanika, Dori, Anie, Sau-Fann, Nevena and so many, many, many more... you know who you are. May you continue to glow **gloriously**, blazing your trail, leaving innumerable masses of awe-struck followers in your **magical** wake.*

Author: Tamara Skyhawk
Copyright: © 2021 by Tamara Skyhawk
Publisher: RTV Yoga Inc. Cover Design: Maryna Nesterchuk
Formatting: Tariq Khan
Icons from Flaticon.com. Artists: PIXARTIST, Freepik, Good Ware, Made by Made Premium, Icongeek26, Frey Wazza, Nikita Golubev, Talha Dogar, BZZRINCANTATION, max.icons

ISBN: 978-1-7774888-9-5 (paperback)
ISBN: 978-1-7777630-3-9 (hardcover)
ISBN: 978-1-7777630-4-6 (e-book)

First Edition 2021

Contents

Mornings 94

Bedtime 104

Author's Note

Hello, gorgeous Queen! I wrote this book to remind you how colossally fabulous, magnificent, strong, beautiful, brilliant and dazzling you are.

These are little pep talks, from one Queen to another, to lift you up when you're facing tough times – a heavy heart, self doubt, social drama, the drudgery of work and housework – the stuff we deal with everyday.

I hope these pep talks make you smile, remind you of how amazing you are and inspire you to celebrate and love all that you are, everyday.

With love,
Tamara

Feelings

Doubting Myself

Queen, do you even *remember* who you are?
The things you've accomplished like a glorious *champion*?
The hardships you've overcome like a warrior *Goddess*?
The grace you've brought to so, so many?
The priceless *treasures* you've birthed into this world,
Ideas,
Creations,
Sensations?
Queen, do you even remember who you ARE??
May I remind you?
You are *absolutely* PHENOMENAL.

Feelings

Not Feeling the Love

Oh my, Queen.
Never you mind.
If you're not feeling the love, just keep moving forward,
Unruffled as ever.
Strut straight ahead, train of magnificence flowing behind you.
No looking back.
No thinking back.
Simply moving on, in the gorgeous, unapologetic way you do.
Unattached.
Undisturbed.
Confident.
Composed.
Doing you, *gloriously*,
Without skipping a beat.

Feeling Old

Oh, Queen.
You are but a fine wine, aged to *perfection!*
Every line,
Every softening,
Every *ounce* of your being holds wildly delicious secrets,
Stories,
Adventures,
And triumphs.
Your legendary appeal has *never* been greater.

Feeling Young

Queen, you have youth on your side.
Never to be underestimated!
You're a firecracker.
Maybe you don't have experience under your gorgeous belt
yet…
But what you lack there, you make up for with electric energy
and joie de vivre.
Never doubt what you bring to the table.
It's a gift – and it doesn't last forever.
Play it up!

Am I Enough?

Pssht. Enough.
Queen, you are a *rainbow* of delights.
A joy in every colour.
The whole spectrum.
A fascination through and through.
Cast your light far and wide.
Cast it daily.
The world needs your *fantastic* array of light.

Am I Too Much?

Queen, you are a WONDER OF THE WORLD.
Do the pyramids question their grandeur?
Does the Mona Lisa question its value?
Does the Taj Mahal question its majesty?
No, Queen.
You are NOT too much.
You are a WONDER OF THE WORLD.
Marvelous.
Captivating.
Wildly extra.

Feeling Unappreciated

Your Grace, can we talk about your grace for a minute?
The constant, magnanimous giving you do,
Gracing others with your talents, love and energy.
Without so much as a thank you or nod of recognition.
May I mention the graceful composure you maintain in the face of that insult.
The grace you embody through *all* hardship and nonsense.
Never doubt your immense worth, Queen.
If someone is not seeing it, know that I see it.
I see you.
And oh, my eyes!
You are a MARVEL.
On behalf of anyone who hasn't said it…
Thank you.

Create/Share That Thing?

Queen, you are MAGNIFICENT.
And with great magnificence comes great responsibility.
You have a *duty* to share your divine expressions with the
world.
The world awaits, Queen.
Awaiting your *outstanding* talents.
Your *extraordinary* vibe.
Your soul-birthed creations.
Let them pour out, unfettered.
Beautiful, unending and *effortlessly* flowing.
Enrapturing as they flow.
In a steady, *spellbinding* stream.

Feelings

Not Feeling Great

Ok, Queen, so you don't feel so hot right now…
No biggie.
We can't see the light without the darkness, right?
Take a rest.
Step by step.
Reset.

Life is Utter Garbage

Queen, this too shall pass.
Pass like the *foul*, stinking offence it is.
Vaporized and dispersed, far, far away from you,
Until not a trace is left near you.
The cloud will disperse,
While you remain.
Fabulous, fragrant, poised as ever.

Feelings

Self-Love

Queen, you bring LIFE.
You're a ray of light.
Soft, glowing, luminous, *divine*.

Feelings

Feeling Like a Failure

Queen, how many times have you fallen?
And aren't you still here?
A fall is nothing but an opportunity to rise again.
Seize it!
Rise up, glorious Queen,
In all your *magnificent* splendor.

Hardship Left and Right

Do you know what you are?
You are a *juicy*, *ripe*, GORGEOUS tomato,
Stuck in the middle of a sh*t sandwich.
Don't let it squeeze your juice, Queen.
You are a *beautifully* plump, resilient tomato.
Nothing's gonna squash you, beauty.

Need to Calm Down

Your Majesty, time for a breather.
Inhale.
Exhale.
There under all the chaos,
Lies your silky, smooth self.

Feeling Kind
of Dumb

Queen, you are a GENIUS...
That beautiful head is full of the most *phenomenal* thoughts,
ideas, notions, and assorted gorgeous whatnot.
Don't you for *a second* doubt it.
You are the BRILLIANCE in brilliant.
You are the SHARP in sharp.
You are the INFINITE in infinite knowledge.
This finite world has no space for your infinite majesty.
You. Are. BRILLIANT.

Feelings

Feeling Fusty

You are a *gorgeous* fresh daisy, Queen.
Look at your dewy, glowing face.
Shimmering and shining.
So pretty. *So* fresh.
So *delightful*!

Let That Sh*t Go

Goodbye.
Good riddance.
Good gracious, *be free*!
A Queen never holds onto anything unworthy.
Stop hoarding that sh*t, tout suite.
It's a filthy devil.
Marring your lovely smile.
Ruining your mood.
Stealing your energy like a despicable thief.
It's unfit to be in your presence.
Banish it NOW.
Lock the gate.
And never let it disturb you again.

Worry and Panic

Queen.
Is this the way you want it to go down?
Let's say the worst happens,
Which we already suspect, won't be as bad as you think.
Do you want all the moments leading up to it to be like this?
Missing all the magical moments, the beauty, the mirth in
what's right in front of you?
Turn your keen, arresting eyes to the beauty all around you.
Look closely.
Can you see it?
Can you smile?
Did the whirling mind stop for a moment?
Can you feel a touch of warmth?
Peace?
The ugly weight of worry dropping from your shoulders like a
heavy royal cape?
Walk forward, light and free.
Keep noticing the beauty.
Revel and rest there.

Feelings

Facing Hardship

You are a ROCK, Queen.
Holding up like the Himalayas.
Solid.
Strong.
Unshakeable.
Majestic and *wild*.

Was That the Right Choice?

Queen, as magnificent and powerful as you are,
You are but one of the stars in the twinkling sky.
There are many forces beyond your control.
Take comfort – there is a greater intelligence at work,
Eternally leading all toward the greater good.

Moving On

Queen, don't you for a *moment* think you're going to settle
here.
This is NOT your new reality.
This is NOT your glowing vibe.
This is NOT the way to spend your precious, *precious* time.
Speak it. Change it. Move ON.
Like the powerful Queen Goddess that you are.
Calling the shots, making the shots.
Don't spend another minute here.
Step those *gorgeous* feet back into the light and keep walking
on, basking in the glorious, radiant light.
That luminous light where you belong.
That luminous light which is the *only* place fit for a Queen.

Feelings

Getting Into a Rut

Queen, did you forget the world is YOUR OYSTER?!
What divine pearl will be next in your *gleaming* collection?
Shake off the old ways.
The heavy.
The dull.
Make space to revel in love with your *new* gem.
The *crown* jewel for your life in this place and this time.

Feeling Beautiful

Mwrrawrrr foxy Queen!
Oh you are FIERCE my dear.
Fiercely *bewitching*.
Make NO mistake.
You. Are. Fierrrrrrrce…

Not Where I Want to Be Yet

Queen, have you seen an acorn?
A cute little acorn?
The *towering* oak tree is in that little package.
All potential is there.
Whatever you think you're *not* right now, you *are*.
It's all wrapped up in adorable seed form.
Just you wait.
Get that acorn in fertile ground.
Water it, water it, WATER IT!
It's *already* in the works,
Beautifully emerging.

Shouldn't
Have Done That

This isn't your first bad choice, Queen.
There have been multitudes.
But you're HERE.
You're reflecting. You're regretting.
Turn that regret into *rejuvenation*.
Turn over a juicy new leaf.
You're growing.
You're blossoming.
And it's a *gorgeous* unfolding.

Starting Over

Two words: PHOE. NIX!!!!
Rise up outta those flames, Queen,
Like the *blazing*, *powerful*, GORGEOUS fine being you are.
Refreshed.
Renewed.
Born again.
Better than ever.
Better than EVER.
Soaring on up to any height you like.
Free and flourishing.
Flying on, flying on.
FLY. ING. *ON*!!!

Feeling Smart

Queen, that wit is *fierce*.
Sharp.
As.
A.
SWORD!

Avoiding
That Thing I Detest

Queen, is that li'l ol' nuisance bothering you again?
Off with it, Majesty.
Where there's a will – and your will is *phenomenal* – there's
certainly a way.
Ditch it… change it… slay it… or pawn it off.
It's greying your glow.
OFF with it!

Feeling Anxious

Queen.
Relax your shoulders.
Relax your jaw.
Sit up regally.
Feel the strength, the power, rise up within you.
Take a walk, floating with grace.
Remember your blessings,
Your accomplishments,
Your creature comforts.
Dive into those and sway with ease.
Breathe with ease.
You are home,
In your peaceful self again.

Juggling Too Much

Feeling overwhelmed, you miraculous minx?
Not surprising.
You *can* do it all, so you often *do*.
But it's too much.
If you need help, ask for help.
No shame, Queen.
You're a leader, not a workhorse.
Even a workhorse deserves the freedom to stay happy.
Request help, Your Majesty.
You're sure to find others eager to help.
And if not, well, put thy royal foot down and demand it!

Work

Going Into a Meeting

Oh, my!
Who *are you*?!!
Can you dim that shine for just a sec, 'cause no one in here can see a thing!
Take a seat and let that brilliance flow out like a gorgeous river of GOLD.
Like a tidal wave.
Any remains of this dusty old place are washed away and you have ushered in the GOLDEN age.
Your ideas are *so* staggering, jaws drop, cannot *wait* to hear more and BASK. IN. THAT. *GOLD.*

Dreaded Paperwork

Queen, yes.
It's a pile of rubbish and nonsense.
But rubbish that none-the-less needs processing.
And who better to do it than you, Your Radiant Brilliance?
At the very least, you could elevate that pile of rubbish.
Gracing it with your signature sparkle.
And next time if it *dare* intrude on your heavenly workspace again,
Banish it to the dungeon!

Messy Workspace

Oh these *trashy* odds and sods.
NO place for them here.
This is *sacred* creative ground for the Queen.
Cast them aside.
Brush aside the dust.
Polish 'til it *gleams* in harmony with your *resplendent* radiance.

Not Taking Enough Breaks

Oh, Queen.
Your efforts are superb.
Your work is astounding.
You deserve equally impressive BREAKS!
Whatever floats your beguiling little boat is fine…
Tea, coffee, treats.
Walking, shopping, dreaming.
Spa, yoga, massage.
You do you.
You've earned it.
Take it.
No apologies.

Eating at My Desk Again

Queen, how pitiful.
Has it come to *this*?
Hunkering down at your desk, shoveling in food like a sad little monkey?
Queen.
Step OUT.
Grace the world with your graceful promenade.
Dine in style.
Treat yourself to the best. Because you ARE the best.
Sad little monkey-hunkering must go.
Let the fine dining, like the fine Queen you are, COMMENCE!

Need to
Do Deep Thinking

Prepare the creative bunker!
High carb foods? Check.
High sugar foods? Check.
Salty, fatty foods? Check.
Splurgealicious treat? Check.
Cozy temperature? Check.
Distractions at bay? Check.
Clothing comfortized? Check.
Release the floodgates!
Let the brilliance FLOW!!

A Job Well Done

YAY, Queen!
Crushin' it, crushin' it,
Crushy, crushy, crushin' it.

Work

Workplace Drama

Oh, Queen.
Your time is *precious*.
Your energy is *priceless*.
And you simply *will not* be dragged into any tactless drama.
A Queen isn't dragged.
She dominates.
She's determined.
Firm.
Unswayed
Unruffled.

Facing a Deadline

A Queen *delivers*.
In your own way.
On your terms.
And at the *precisely* perfect time.
You *consistently* deliver your genius.
And *selflessly* share your gifts.
This will be no exception.
The accolades, await.

Making a Presentation

Hello, powerful FIERCENESS.
I can hear you roaring and you haven't even opened your mouth yet.
Time to unleash that devastating brilliance, Queen.
Deliciously savage and *stunning*.

Not the Most Exciting Task

Oh sweet Queen…
Not everything sparkles like you.
Some things are dull, drab and boring.
Bring the *shine*, Queen!
Light it up like only you do, Ms. Midas.
Bring the GOLD.
Bring the glow.
Bring the *fabulosity*.
If ever there was something that needed it, it's this.
And it needs you NOW.

Work

Avoiding
That Project

Queen, are you telling me you're afraid of a little ol' project?
For realsies, it's probably more afraid of you.
Look at it cowering in the shadow of your *devastating*
brilliance and might.
Might you take that mighty might and just get in there?
This is going to be a *cinch* for Your Highness.
We all already know it.
Just get in there and exalt that thing to the *height* of heights,
Like the *extraordinary* Empress of Work that you are.

Procrastinating

Queen, did you forget how *valuable* your time is?
Priceless.
Like the *spectacular* gem that you are.
If you're tired, then take your royal rest.
If you're overwhelmed, grace just one thing with your royal
attention, and cast aside the rest.
You *are* the Queen, darling.
But do NOT waste your *extraordinary* wit texting, scrolling and
loafing.
Pour your resplendent brilliance into just one task.
Let it shine as a *dazzling* example of your might and gloriosity.
One thing is *more* than enough.
What a treasured *gift* it will be for the world.

Still Procrastinating

Darling, *stop* reading.
Get started.
GET THIS OFF YOUR GORGEOUS BACK!!
You'll smash it like you do everything else.
And in no time you'll be floating free again, in your signature
sublime and *spectacular* bubble of bliss.

Celebrating Success

And the award goes to…
You, Queen!
Once again… perfection.
Magical.
Brilliant.
A thunderous roar of applause to you, Your Majesty, for yet
another *masterful* accomplishment.

Changing Jobs/Career

Queen, your gorgeous boots were made for *walking on*.
You *cannot* be contained here anymore.
You are bubbling forth, ready to explode in a dazzling shower
of brilliance.
Clear the way. Cut the ties.
Your freedom is imminent.

Home

Cleaning the House

Queen, this is your PALACE.
Time to get in there and sweep up this *nonsense*.
You deserve a sparkling, shining, *gorgeous* abode for your gorgeous self.

Home

Paying Bills

Oh, the heaviness of a bill.
So dull and mundane.
Finish it quickly.
It's dimming your radiance.

Doing Taxes

Oh, throw them a bone my dear.
How pitifully they beg for a pittance of your illustrious
fortune.
If they only knew where your true riches lie…

That Broken Thing

Queen, please.
Fix it, give it to someone who can, or move on.
It's a fright for sore eyes.

Home

Stained/Tattered Clothing

Seriously?
Queen, that garb is *garbage*.
Will you adorn your majestic bod with rubbish?
Into the bin.
Less is more, Your Royal Highness.

Home

Need to Clean That Drawer

Queen.
When did this *junk* drawer creep up in here?
No *thank* you.
Rubber bands? Uh… ok, useful.
Random phone number? Gone.
Receipts? Buh-bye.
Broken thing – woop woo – in the trash we go.
Fork – not mine, and wrong drawer.
Batteries – Google recycling.
Buttons – what are those for?
Leaky pen – *ugh*.
Queen, this is going to feel *so* good when you're done.
Keep going.
This junky drawer has *no* place in your royal abode.
Press on.
Off with the dregs.

Home

Editing
My Wardrobe

Oh, Queen.
Some of these rags are *dangerous*!
Are you going to let them keep soiling your image?
Queen.
Toss them or give them away.
They're distracting you from the finer apparel.
If it isn't sparking joyful exaltation, it isn't fit for a Queen.
Onward and upward, draped in only the best.
Your edited wardrobe eagerly anticipates adorning your
exquisite body.

Home

Laundry Day

Time to wash off the funk of the mundane world, Queen.
Start *afresh*, free and clear.
Pristine.
Fragrant.
Beautified.
Ready to re-enter the common world again,
Restored to your regal purity,
Enrobed in a halo of laundered freshness.

Home

Doing Dishes

Your Majesty,
You must approach this from an elevated perspective.
Think not of the grime of meals past, but the
sensuality of the task.
The flowing water.
Luxuriant bubbles.
Sparkling cleanliness.
A 5-star dishwashing experience is in your hands.

Home

Social

Going on a Date

Elegant.
Engaging.
Irresistible.
Terrifying charm,
Ravishing beauty,
Set to swoon.
Please be gentle.
Have *mercy*!

Thank That Person

Queen, don't be a buffoon.
It's beneath you.
Give thanks-a-plenty and give it now.

Make Actual Plans

Remember when you said, "let's get together"?
Be real, Your Highness.
Your integrity depends upon it.
And you'll feel better seeing that friend.
Even a Queen needs confidantes.
Especially a Queen.

Social

Meeting
New People

Oh, the opportunity!
Gorgeous new alliances.
Sharing your magnificence.
Standing firm in your worth.
At ease, yet en garde, should an unwelcome intruder cause
your beautiful brow to furrow.
In that case, move *swiftly* along.
Time waits for no brow-furrower.
On to find delightful *new* allies.

A Friend Lost Her Self-Love

Be a friend, Queen.
Lift her to the *summit* of self-esteem, as only YOU can.
Guide her to the pinnacle of self-confidence –
Your eternal abode.
Let her see herself as she never has, but as you do.
Show her her blinding magnificence.

Hosting a Party

Your Excellence, it's time to cause a *right* royal rumpus.
Let's get this soiree started, and *SOON!*
Mischief, intrigue, glory, flamboyance…
Rogues, beautiful ones and ne'er do wells.
A cocktail for mayhem, laughter, romance,
With you Queen, presiding as Mistress of Ceremonies.

Formal Event

Glamour.
Presence.
Dressed to the NINES.
Striking.
Statement.
Looking FINE!

Social

Everyday

Taking Time for Me

Who is the most important person in your kingdom?
It's *you*, Your Excellence.
Without you, there *is* no kingdom.
Swear allegiance to the Queen, above all else.
You have a duty to take care of indubitably irreplaceable you.
And don't forget to do it with style, decadence and all the
dazzle due to a legendary Queen.

Everyday

Too Tired to Wash My Face

Lather up that visage, Queen!
It's a priceless treasure.
And *you* are its caretaker.
Caress it.
Anoint it.
Let it know without a shadow of a doubt, that
IT
IS
LOVED.

Cooking Dinner — Again

Queen, you deserve to dine without dimming.
If you detest it, delegate it!
Enjoy a sumptuous feast,
Without lifting a lovely little finger.

That Doesn't Fit Anymore

Queen, it's not *you*, it's the garment.
Give it away and move on.
It's a drag unfit for your latest stunning incarnation.
Float forward, unfettered.

Nothing
Fits Anymore

Wheee!!
Time to slip into a brand *spanking* new wardrobe, fit for a
QUEEN.
NO expense spared for Your Royal Highness.
Your beauty *must not* be dimmed by these ill-fitting *rags*.

Taking Time to Relax

Queen, lay that beautiful body down.
It's time for Your Highness to rest, refresh and *renew*.
Renew, like the dewy, ripe berry you are.
Fresh and irresistibly juicy.
You are here for you.
This is *your* special time.
Just for you.
You are entitled to treat yourself to every little thing you need
right now to be supremely comfortable.
Fluffy pillow, cozy blankie, beautiful scent.
Anything you need.
Get yourself every little thing that makes your heart sing in
sweet relaxation.
Red carpet laid out for you to embark on this gorgeous
journey of relaxation.
Let the nonsense and noise fall away.
No space for that here.
You are fully filling this space.
Infinite, boundless, limitless.
And you do it so, *so* effortlessly.
Completely effortless.

Everyday

Just you and your remarkable self.
Nothing to do.
Sinking in.
Effortless.
Gorgeously sublime.
Effortless.
Let your beautiful awareness sail on.
Body resting.
Floating gracefully on to awareness of your breath.
Your incredible body, breathing itself.
Nothing else to do but rest in your sweet self.

Your Majesty… if you'd like further sweet relaxation, feast thy fine eyes on my book: Yoga Nidra Scripts: 22 Meditations for Effortless Relaxation, Rejuvenation and Reconnection.

Everyday

Start That Thing
I Love, Again

Queen, do you remember the joy?
The pure *joy*.
Joy for joy's sake.
Doing that thing you love?
Do you remember?
It was FABULOSITY.
Heart-exploding, maddeningly happy, giddy…
So sweet you wanna squeeze it.
Essence of life, essence of your soul.
Soul exploding fireworks in your chest.
The food of love.
PLAY ON.

Everyday

A Long To-do List

Look at you – taking care of business, like a boss!
Check, check, *check*.
SLAYING that to-do list.
Powering through like a BEAST.
So powerful,
So swift,
Tackling it all with ease and *breathtaking* grace.
You are a Queen who gets things DONE.

Everyday

Want to Eat Healthier

Queen, your body is a GODDESS TEMPLE.
Don't worship by bringing junk.
Bring the best.
The freshest.
The sweetest.
The juiciest.
The richest – in vitamins, minerals, goodness for the
GODDESS.
Only the best.
For the best.

Everyday

Need to
Get to Bed Earlier

Beauty sleep, beautiful Queen.
And not only that, but a refresh for your gorgeous mind.
Wake up ready to thrill and amaze in your magical way.
A blessing for you, and *all*.
Now slip into those sheets, Queen!

Everyday

Cultivating Gratitude

Queen, you are *so* fortunate.
You have *SO much* others would love to have.
Remember it.
Treasure it.
Share it.
Be grateful, grateful, *GRATEFUL.*
And please keep your head out of your royal butthole.

Stop That Bad Habit

Can't you see it, Majesty?
That bad habit is constantly stalking you.
Clinging to you like a leech.
Guzzling away your enchanting effervescence.
Draining.
Dulling.
Dastardly.
Slay it now, like the *fierce* warrior Goddess you are.
No mercy for the wicked.

Everyday

Keep Up
That Good Habit

You are MIGHTY.
Building a new habit is no easy feat.
While the faint of heart would have faltered, you persisted,
dominating any challenge.
A habit shapes character.
Character shapes destiny.
You have set a course for exciting new discoveries,
experiences, realities.
Continue the crusade, Queen.
Your new world awaits.

Everyday

Dressed Up,
Ready to Go

Queen, where did you get the *AUDACITY* to be looking so *fine*
on this fine day?!
It's *OUTRAGEOUS*!
Well done!

Everyday

Get on My Yoga Mat

Show that beautiful body some LOVE!
Cultivate the peace, health, *vibrance* fit for a Queen.
Thy gorgeous toes, fingers and derriere grace thy mat.
What a blessing to all.
Queen, this is your time for you.
Don't miss this chance to breathe in the *heavenly* experience of
your sublime self – body, mind and soul.

Everyday

Drink More Water

Queen, you are an exquisite bloom that must be watered, and watered *well*.
Drink up, Diva!

Everyday

Need to Exercise

Time to *luxuriate* in feel-good hormones.
A rush of endorphins.
A flush in your cheeks.
Glistening, dewy skin and blood throbbing through your veins.
Oh! Be still your beating heart, Queen.
You are on FIRE when you exercise!

Everyday

Desperately Need Pampering

Queen, this is a *three* bath day.
With all the fizzies, bubbles, oils, and cotton candy.
Not one, not two, but *three* baths.
For *luxy* little you.
Your Juicy Highness.
Soaking in this shameless indulgence,
For your *sparkling* self.

Everyday

Seasonal

Spring Cleaning

Dusty sad things? *No.*
Trying to be something you're not things? *No.*
Old self things? *No.*
New self things? Yes, ma'am.
Remnants of old lovers? Hello... *Goodbye.*
Ill-fitting clothes? Toss. Toss. Toss.
Tarnished jewels? No thank you.
Favourite sweater? Yes please.
Cute pic from your past? Bring that into *the light*!
Brilliant creative project? Front. And. Centre.
YOU. ARE. REFRESHED!!

Seasonal

Spring Season Approaching

Get ready, Queen…
The season of rebirth, refresh, reimagine is on the way!
What will your new incarnation look like this year?
Blossoming out like a gorgeous, bright bloom.
Bringing beauty to all.
Joy to all.
Wonder.
Can you feel the energy lightening?
Lifting off like a pretty balloon?
Light as air, you float through your days, with a happy whirl
and a carefree spirit.
Oh, Queen, imagine it.
It's on the way.

Seasonal

Summer Season Approaching

Hello, Queen.
The season to match your hotness is arriving.
Time to drop the coverings and reveal that gorgeous skin!
Beautiful, soft, glistening in the sun.
Hot, hot, HOT!
Sunshine, this is your chance to *shine*.
Bring the boldness.
Bring the blaze.
Bring the brilliance.
You are on FIRE!

Seasonal

Fall Season Approaching

Queen, that cozy little season of fall is coming.
Shed what you no longer need.
And bundle up in comfort.
Slow down.
Appreciate.
Let go.

Winter Season Approaching

Queen, Jack Frost nips at your nose, but your soul is *toasty*.
Battened down, cozy cool, ready for your royal *rest*.
Hold your calls.
Cancel your appointments.
The royal rest is about to COMMENCE.
You go on right ahead and get yourself every little thing you
need to hi. ber. *nate*.
Cozy blankies.
Fluffy socks.
Silky sheets.
Bubbly baths.
'Tis the season for your beau. ty. *rest*!

Seasonal

Mornings

Morning
Look in the Mirror

Hello, dreamy.
You are looking *so* fine.
Like an angelic Dorian Gray –
With each good deed, your reflection becomes *more* beautiful.
It's a *whole* new level of beauty today.
Beautiful thoughts.
Beautiful face.
Beautiful deeds sprinkled *all* over your world today.
Like a magic fairy dusting your little sparkle wand of
sweetness all over this world.
Oh yes, Your Royal Magic Fairy.
This is some majestic sparkle about to grace the world today.

Rainy Morning

Your Excellence…
A damp, dark morning awaits beyond these, thy royal covers.
You must trudge forward…
Those on the frontlines will need your lustrous light today.
Summon your strength and align with the allure of this day…
The sublime quiet, the soft, diffused light.
Float like the dream that you are, lighting the way for yourself
and your people.
God-speed in this, your gentle mission.

Sunny Morning

What a vision!
You.
The sunshine.
Possibility.
Adventure.
A new day dawning.
Step out into the light, gorgeous Queen!

Cold Morning

Get your HOT self out of bed.
There's a cold front and we need your *sizzling* self on the front lines.
Melt it, Queen!

Hot Morning

Set it to chill-mode, Queen.
Your royal hotness is too much for today.
Have mercy!

Mornings

Luxy Day

Luxe, luxe, luxe…
What will it be today?
A luxury of time?
A luxury of generosity?
A luxury of loving?
A luxury of beauty?
A luxury of talent?
A luxury of care?
What flavour will your luxe life be today?

Mornings

Everyday
Celebration

Every day is a chance to celebrate.
To unbox a new toothpaste tube.
To use a favourite, fragrant soap.
To revel in the freshness of a just-cleaned room.
To plan an adventure.
To appreciate someone.
To tick off some of your to-do list.
To lie down and relax for a while, doing nothing.
To laugh with your favourite comedian.
To plan a sweet surprise for someone.
To eat something delicious.
To gaze at the sky.
To put on a favourite pyjama.
To slip into cool sheets at the end of the day.
To find beauty in every day.

Mornings

Morning Tiredness

Queen, if you need to rest, then rest.
Stand firm, lying down.
The Queen's needs have been stated and *must* be followed.

May I suggest, Your Sleeping Beauteousness, if the tiredness persists day after day, do look into the nuisance causing it and use your substantial royal wit to affect change. It's a blight on your otherwise dazzling existence.

Average Morning

Good morning, you *exquisite* creature.
What beauty will blossom forth from you today?
What light will you bring?
What joy?
What wisdom?
What *mischief*?
Shake off the night.
Shake up a *gorgeous* new day.

Bedtime

Restless Bedtime

Oh, Queen.
So sorry to hear restlessness has kidnapped your
beautiful brain.
Have you written down any worries or to-do items yet?
Sometimes it helps to put them – and you – to rest.
Screens off?
Bedtime bath?
Quiet? Dark?
Done a few stretches?
Soothing meditation?
Counted the things you're grateful for?
Wishing you a sweet slumber.
And if not, rest assured your terrific might will carry you
through the next day anyway.

*Majesty, may I suggest... Yoga Nidra (an effortless meditation) can help with sleep. Enjoy
some of my Yoga Nidra recordings for free, at tamaraskyhawk.com/free.*

Bedtime

Bedtime Lullaby

Hush-a-bye and goodnight,
Go to sleep gorgeous Queen.
You're a marvel. You're a doll.
You're a sizzling siren, too.
Go to sleep, gorgeous Queen,
In the morning, you'll astonish.
Go to sleep, gorgeous Queen.
In the morn, you'll amaze.

Hard Day Bedtime

Undeniably a rough one today.
Your strength is *so* impressive.
So admirable.
And now,
All the holding up, bearing and strength,
Can fall away,
Take a rest,
Recharge.
As you fall into effortless sleep.
No effort needed now, whatsoever.
Let any tension fall away.
Shedding.
Softening.
Sleeping.

Accomplished Day Bedtime

What an awe-inspiring day!
Wondrous.
Astonishing.
Only possible for a true Queen.
And now,
May you fall weightlessly into your well-deserved rest.
Sweet dreams, sensational Queen.

Lovely Bedtime

Oh, sweet Queen, I love you.
I love who you are.
I love how you are.
I love what you do.
I'm so lucky to be you.
I love everything about you.
Sweet dreams, gorgeous being.

Reviews
Appreciated!

Enjoy the book?
Sharing a review on Amazon is *amazingly* helpful. More
Queens will discover the book and be lifted to ecstatic new
heights of self-love and magnificence.

Look at you empowering other Queens – as you *ever* do,
Your Majesty.

Leave your review on Amazon now!

Thanks, Queen!
Tamara

Other Books
by Tamara Skyhawk

Yoga Nidra Scripts
22 Meditations for Effortless Relaxation,
Rejuvenation and Reconnection

Yoga Nidra Scripts 2
22 More Meditations for Effortless Relaxation,
Rejuvenation and Reconnection

Yoga Nidra-Skripte
22 Meditationen für Mühelose Entspannung,
Verjüngung und Wiederverbindung

Are You a Tomato?
A Silly, Interactive Book to Help Kids Build
Confidence in Their Self-Identity and Resilience to Bullying

Come Out and Play
A Kids' Book to Inspire a Love of Nature and Outdoor Play

All available on Amazon.
Learn more about these and upcoming books and courses at
tamaraskyhawk.com.

Made in the USA
Las Vegas, NV
06 November 2023

80345780R00068